What clien r:

I would like to §   *irds to*
her organizatio   *luable*
volunteer here ._ .....,, \u0441nur\u0441n at The Fountains, Stafford,
Texas. One of her accomplishments included the organization of
our resource room making it a more efficient and feasible work
area for other volunteers. Lisa also has made a significant change
and improvement in our storage room, which includes supplies,
maintenance equipment, and documentation. Among these she
also leads in our attendance, care groups, and hospitalization
visitation team.

Steve Castillo, Pastor
Stafford, TX

Lisa Giesler has always shown supreme organizational skills. She comes by it naturally. For someone who does not flow in that area she came as a wonderful gift to me in my time of need. We began with my closets. She also helped in getting ready for my move including preparing for a garage sale and packing. The way she packed also made things easier. She encouraged me to put aside what I didn't need. It took a load off to know I wasn't packing unnecessary and was also able to donate and receive a tax write off. These were all a blessings.

Tina Boyd, Secretary, Believer's Life Family Church
New Orleans, LA

Thank you so much for helping me organize my home office and
my closet. You make organizing so fun and easy. Did I mention we
accomplished this only in a few short hours, and it was absolutely
painless? Now, both rooms look great and I have a place to put
everything. Now, maintaining is almost effortless.

Mandy Kao
Missouri City, TX

Lisa's energy and passion for what she does is always refreshing. It is wonderful to find someone who is not only talented at what she does but genuinely cares about her clients. She organized my office after finding out not only my needs but finding out more about my personality. There is not a "cookie cutter" solution when Lisa comes into a project. She customizes each job based on the client's needs and personality. I would recommend her to anyone for personal or business organization.

Kelli Smith, Signature Promotions
Missouri City, TX

Lisa, thank you for organizing my office. I really appreciated the organizing last year and this year was even better! It was just the extra organization I needed, to be able to get so much more accomplished. I think that every business should have an organizer come once a year for maintenance. I know we definitely will!!! Thank You,

Glenn Guidry, President, La Maison Creole
Harvey, LA

It just so happened, as all good things do in a perfectly aligned universe, that my phone rang and just like a cheerful and magical fairy Godmother; there appeared Lisa Giesler. Now, yall know I am not organized. I couldn't possibly find any point to being so, what with all the artsy and albeit "more important" tasks at hand. Nana used to say "there's a place for everything... and everything should be in its place", and lo and behold you'll never guess the slogan that Lisa has..."A Time and Place for Everything!" ...for the first time thanks to Lisa Giesler I can find anything!

Alisa Murray, Alisa Murray Photography
Missouri City, TX

Who doesn't promise to clear the chaos and clutter out of their lives each January with the best of intentions? I know I do...No one likes mess, whether it's at our home or at the office. Well, this year I decided to do something about it! I hired Lisa Giesler of A Time and Place for Everything. I was so overwhelmed I never used my home office. It was a holding room for all things misplaced. She came in cheerfully and took over. It was done and all filed away in one day, whew! It is now a place of solace that I can retreat to when I need to pay bills, write or just be at peace. I cannot thank you enough!!! You make it so easy and fun...

Lisa Fredrickson, Publisher, Fort Bend Focus Magazine
Sugarland, TX

I first heard Lisa speak at a WCR luncheon last year and was just blown away. She made everyone feel as though they are just having a conversation with a very good friend. Her energy and enthusiasm is contagious. Lisa makes everything seem fun, even getting rid of clutter. I've had her come and help me organize my office and I am still on track because of the tips she gave me. Lisa has a passion for what she does and it is exemplified in everything she does.

Thomasine Johnson, Principal, En'terior Designs
Houston, TX

Lisa spoke to a lovely group a few months ago, and I was lucky enough to be her guest. She did an awesome job. She was very organized in her thoughts and left the women wanting more. She provoked quite a question and answer session after she was finished, not to mention, one of the women who had used her services gave rave reviews on her talents as a professional organizer!

Pamela Lockard, Marketing
Richmond, TX

Knowledgeable in the art of organizing, Lisa breaks it down so that keeping yourself physically as well as spiritually in order seems so simple. You'll love Lisa's sense of humor, her transparency, and her ability to make you walk away confidently feeling like "I can do this!"

Pastor Dena Trice, Maranatha Church
Mont Belvieu, TX

3

Lisa came to my home to help me with many organizational problems from my kitchen cabinets to office supplies to toys for three children. Not only did we get everything organized, but Lisa was also able to give me some pointers to help me maintain order and organize myself in the future. My husband and I were both extremely pleased with the work she did in our home (my husband sings her praises to this day). -- We cannot thank you enough Lisa!

K M
Sugar Land, TX

"Lisa is amazing! After moving into a new home a little over a year ago, I asked Lisa to come take a look at my home office. The hardest part about moving is figuring out where to put things, and I was in despair because our previous home had a closet in my home office where I could store things out of sight. Now I had things that I didn't know what to do with or where to put them. Lisa came in, and in no time at all, had my home office brilliantly organized and all my "piles" off the floor. She used storage solutions that I never would've thought about on my own. Our time together was used very efficiently, because she brought her assistant who went out and purchased storage containers while we stayed home and worked. Now my office has never looked better and I am so relieved!"

Karen Steede-Terry
Author of Full Time Woman Part Time Career

"Lisa is a master at bringing order to chaos. After a recent move, I was too tired and overwhelmed to organize my office. She came in and we worked together to get everything up and running! I am forever grateful. Without her, I might still be in boxes."

Nancy Olson

Since Lisa Giesler came to speak, women have said that they learned tips and are now getting organized. Her presentation was inclusive and encouraging.

Sugar Land, Aglow International

4

I never thought that I needed an organizer, and never dreamed that I would use one, until I was introduced to Lisa Giesler. When Lisa arrived at my home, she was completely ready to tackle the jobs that I had left undone for years. The back closet that was never given any attention all of a sudden was transformed into a truly useful room, and many treasures were found that I had not seen in years.

Lisa has a special way of teaching you the skills of organization, as she creatively transforms your home or business into a place of order. This was not just a cleaning exercise, but one of organizing and redistribution. Lisa was able to help me see things through her eyes, knowing what to keep and what was best to let go of. She is truly a gifted individual, and her team is also amazing. My entire home is now a stress free zone because I can find anything that I need to quickly. Everything is properly labeled and pleasing to look at.

After working with Lisa, I am convinced that she can and will transform your home or office into an organized and beautiful place to be, adding her special talents of design.

MaryAnn Markarian
SugarLand, TX

MY LIFE IS A MESS

ORGANIZING 101

MY LIFE IS A MESS

A MESS

ORGANIZING 101

Lisa Giesler

LUCIDBOOKS

My Life is a Mess

Acknowledgments

Thank you to:

My husband, Joseph, for releasing me to complete this project. This has been a dream in my heart for 20 years.

My son, Joseph, for helping to keep the computer up and running and taking care of the groceries for me.

My son, Charles, for being my writer for this book and my business assistant.

My sister, Judy Pastor, for being my cheerleader.

The many businesses in Fort Bend County, Texas, for giving wisdom and taking me under their wing when I was a new business owner.

Foreword

"Stop the world - let me off", is the cry of so many today. Their world is full of days that overwhelm them due to the vast amount of tasks facing them. A seemingly endless demand for their time with no end in sight.

Lisa Giesler is answering the cry! Lisa has a unique gift. The ability to help others "Redeem the Time".

Lisa will walk with you page by page, enabling you to reach the place you've been searching for. Organized and de-cluttered with a fresh focus on life.

At the end of your journey you will shout, "I'm free at last!"

Richard Ford
Senior Pastor
Family Worship Center
Stafford, Texas

Introduction
Not Just Another Book on Organization

This book is inspired to be a basic tool with easy and simple instructions for the person beginning to get organized. It is not filled with the latest technology and details on organizing. This book contains tips such as "put it away" and questions to ask yourself when it may be time to "get rid of things". Its purpose is to free you from the stress of clutter and teach you simple organizing techniques to get organized and stay organized.

When I was young, I was the neat one in the family. I was called the "White Tornado" and not always affectionately. Whenever a family member could not find an item, I was the one to blame. Who would have thought that putting cereal back in the pantry was a crime? Someone would tell me, "Leave the baggies on the table. I might need them." I would sarcastically reply, "Oh yeah? When…like next Tuesday?"

I tried to make this book fun and easy to read by including personal stories with simple and practical tips that you can begin using immediately. Also, I have provided work pages that will help you make notes and develop your own organizing goals. The ultimate purpose of this book is that the reader is able to find the time and place for the things that matter.

How much is clutter costing you?

According to Internet studies, the average person can lose up to 2 hours a day as a result of disorganization. People spend a lot of time looking for receipts, shoes, or keys. If you are losing time at home because of disorganization, then these habits can carry over to your job and other areas of your life.

I had a client who claimed that she "knew where everything was." When I helped her to de-clutter and get her home organized, she found a check from a now-closed account that was worth thousands. The check had been buried in a pile of unopened mail and other paperwork that had been collecting for years. What should have taken 10 or 15 minutes to run by the bank to make a quick deposit now took hours to correct. The pile also contained invitations to networking meetings and business leads that had been missed and were now worthless. The pile was a vivid testament to lost sales opportunities.

People often find clutter overwhelming. If a person tends to save things that they "might" need, then clutter will start to accumulate. Those piles continue to grow until that person can no longer find the thing they "might" have needed in the first place.

I recently organized some of my church's closets. As I discovered buried treasures, a question came to mind. How much money had been spent replacing these beautiful and certainly forgotten items? When it came time to decorate the church for Christmas, I was able to save the church several hundred dollars by recovering those tucked-away decorations.

How many times have you made a repeat purchase because you couldn't find what you were looking for or didn't remember you had it? Have you ever paid a penalty for a late bill? Are you ready to find everything in your home or office?

Chapter 1
Evaluating Your Time

Need to do, should do, and want to do

In the mornings do you feel rushed when you are getting ready? Do you feel as if you are trying to beat the clock as you: make breakfast, clean the kitchen, get the kids ready for school, locate notes for today's meeting, and look for a clean shirt to wear? Are your evenings increasingly chaotic? Do you find yourself running kids to baseball practice or dance classes, helping kids get homework done, and trying to figure out what's for dinner?

There seems to be so many "need to do's," "should do's," and "want to do's," but not enough time to do them. As an organizer, I've noticed that wanting to get organized usually goes hand in hand with finding the time to get organized.

Some people need helping organizing their schedules first and then they are ready for help in organizing their homes and offices. Other people know how to get organized; they just don't have the time to get organized. I had a client call me to help her get organized. In our first appointment, she asked me if I could organize her schedule before I helped her organize the house. This woman was a full-time working mom; her daughter was involved in the scouts, and she was the den mom, the sectional mom, the district mom, and the day camp mom. Her son decided he now wanted to be in scouts and wanted her to be his scout volunteer mom too. With her very busy schedule, she complained that the house was a mess, she couldn't find her notes for the scout training session, and they were going to have to eat fast food every night because she wouldn't have time to fix anything. She couldn't figure out how to organize her life, much less her home. She wanted help.

The first thing we did was evaluate her current schedule. When we physically wrote down what she was doing, we were able to see where her time was being used. We repurposed her time for either productivity or relaxation. Here are 10 easy steps we used to evaluate her schedule:

Tips for evaluating your schedule:

1. Write down what a typical day looks like, including the weekends.
2. How long does it take to for you to get ready in the morning?
3. How long does it take the children to get ready in the morning?
4. How much time do you have for lunch at work and do you have time to work on any personal tasks?
5. What activities do you have in the evenings?
6. What chores could you delegate to the older children, husband, or friend?
7. What kind of meals are you and your family eating and could you create a list of quick and healthy meal options?

8. Which volunteer activities are the most important to you and which ones could you pass on to another volunteer?
9. Make a list of things that you would like to accomplish. List anything from cleaning a closet to getting your nails done.
10. Journal yourself for a few days. Record everything you do and how long it takes. This is a good gauge to see how you are really spending your time.

After we evaluated her schedule, we then set up her new calendar with check lists of projects that she wanted to accomplish. I showed her how she could: delegate some of the household chores to her older children, work on special projects during her lunch time, and pass on some of the volunteering to another mom. She realized that she had more time to enjoy her family. She even said "Now, I can volunteer for more things!" I didn't recommend it. The important point was that now she had time for the things that mattered.

With our multiple roles and ever-increasing schedules, many women feel that they can't do it all. By applying the tips that you have read, you will be empowered to make decisions that will enable you to enjoy your home and your life.

Worksheet

Do you identify with the situation described in this chapter?

_____

_____

_____

_____

_____

_____

If yes, then evaluate your own schedule?

_____

_____

_____

_____

What do you see in your schedule that could be improved?

_____

_____

_____

_____

_____

_____

Chapter 2
Nothing Accomplished

Things that steal our time

Have you ever felt at the end of the day, that although you had the best of intentions, you accomplished nothing? It's often the little distractions or interruptions that eat away our time. Here is a list of possible things that can steal your time and how you can address each issue.

Telephone

I had a friend who would call and sometimes I would say, "I can't talk, I have to go…" but she would not stop talking and to let me speak. Her calls were very time consuming. I do not believe in dodging all personal calls, but they do take time. We would never make personal phone calls on a business phone during work hours, but the same rule should apply to the home-school mom, home-based business person or college student. If you have a first priority then you need to take care of that during that time period.

Tips for saving time on the telephone:

- Caller ID allows you to answer calls that you need to take and delay those you can return later. Note: If you are the caller and someone doesn't answer; leave a complete message and then make note that you left a message to avoid repeated calls.
- Listen to your voice mails, and if you need to return the call and time is limited, use a timer and get to the point quickly.
- Texting allows you to send a specific message quickly and by-passes the time-consuming chatter. I love chatting, but there isn't always time for it.

Emails and Online Social Networking

I received a call from a potential insurance agent (I was waiting for that call). The agent gave me a price quote for my home and auto insurance. When I hung the phone up, I decided to check an email message that contained the insurance quote comparison from my original agent. When I opened my email, there was a message from my husband (it was a hysterically funny joke). I forwarded it to a friend. I couldn't resist the urge to call my friend and let her know I'd sent her the joke. After leaving a message on her voice mail, I washed some laundry. I suddenly remembered that I got so caught up in the joke that I had forgotten to check the email for the insurance quote. I went back and completed the task. Before the insurance agent called I'd been working on a speech I was giving for a meeting that night on, of all things, Time Management and Getting Organized. I had just wasted an hour.

Tips for saving time on the computer:

- Set aside 2 or 3 times a day to check email or social networking sites
- Schedule a fixed amount of time (such as 15 minutes) to check email and set your timer
- Review the subject line of each email to determine its importance and urgency
- Flag the important ones that you need to follow-up on in order of importance
- Avoid reading trivial emails; you may want to forward them to your personal email account or to a folder to read when you have more time.

Multiple Projects

Sometimes you will be faced with multiple projects having multiple deadlines. It may be unproductive to try to work on all of them at once without having a specific plan. If you have formed a habit of bouncing between projects like this, then you may be losing time and focus.

Tips for working on multiple projects:

- For multiple projects, determine the amount of time that you will spend on each project or tasks and set a timer to avoid losing track of time.
- If you have more than one project that needs attention, before you switch tasks, work to an appropriate stopping point and document where you left off. This will prevent you from spending unproductive time trying to figure out where you left off and where you will resume the previous project.

- Try to leverage your time on all of your projects by identifying similar tasks related to them all and work on those together.
- Keep track of when each project is due to avoid missing any deadlines.

Planning and Preparation

Never underestimate the value of planning. Steve had a quarterly meeting on his calendar that he was expected to lead. He scheduled the meeting, but completely forgot to take the time to prepare his notes. The day of the meeting arrives and he "wings it." Steve is not happy that he forgot to bring up some key points, but he figured that no one would notice. Once Steve returned to his seat, his co-worker whispered in his ear, "That was pretty good for winging it." Steve's co-worker had noticed. Steve's meeting was unsuccessful because he did not properly prepare. If he had scheduled the time to prepare for his presentation, then it would have been a success. He thought no one would notice, but they did. This is often the case in situations like these. It is easy to write off responsibilities or just "wing it," but it is even easier to schedule time to prepare, then you will have the satisfaction of knowing that your responsibilities are handled as planned.

Tips for planning a meeting or project:

1. Write the date when the project or meeting is due on your calendar.
2. Schedule time to gather the needed resources or prepare notes.
3. Make extra copies of the agenda for those in attendance.

4. Have the time and place of where the meeting will be held, be sure to arrive a few minutes early to review your notes.

Networking/social gatherings

When I first started my own business, I looked forward to every social networking opportunity that I could attend. In pursuit of those events, I began to realize that some of my other responsibilities were slipping and that the cost of attending these events was climbing. I had to develop a more efficient plan for networking and socializing.

Tips for business networking and social gatherings:

- Find out who will be attending the meeting and what will the subject matter be; carefully consider if the cost of this event is advantageous to you or your business.
- Decide if you really have time in your schedule to attend. Plan your activities by scheduling which events would be beneficial or pique your interest.
- Once you are at the event, pay attention to the time so that you do not stay too late. It is important to keep to your schedule.
- If there is someone you would like to visit with longer, then set up a follow-up time to meet with them after the event.

Distraction or fatigue

On occasion, I find myself worrying or preoccupied at night or during a meeting. When that happens, I have difficulty focusing because I am thinking of other things that I need to do. My sleep is not productive and neither is my time in the meeting. To manage this time more effectively, someone once gave me the following advice:

Tips if you are distracted:

- If you remember a phone call that needs to be made, then stop and jot it down. Sometimes just writing it down will take the load off your shoulders. You can then continue working and address the phone call later.
- If you feel you can't sleep because you are preoccupied about a morning meeting, get up and write some of your thoughts down. It may seem like getting out of bed to write down your thoughts will only waste more time that could be spent sleeping, but practicing this will actually put your mind at ease. You will be much more efficient in the morning if you get a good night's sleep, and the simplest way to take things off your mind is to put them on paper.
- Make sure you leave your note in a location you will see later or the next day. When I am away from home, I send myself an email from my phone. This way I don't have to worry about remembering to look at my notebook.

In the early days of my business, I would often work until late at night and feel completely exhausted the next day. Before I hired a book keeper, I did my own accounting. The summer had been incredibly busy, and at night, I would work late on my books. When I finally had the book keeper come and reconcile my books, we found that I'd made careless errors because I had been exhausted. Sometimes when a person has been working on a certain project or reading for an extended period of time, fatigue sets in.

Tips for preventing fatigue:

- When you realize that you are tired, stop and take a break.
- You may want to go outside or get a change of scenery for a while.
- Eating healthy snacks will help you keep up your energy.

After taking a break, you can come back refreshed and energized with new ideas. To continue working when you are tired not only results in a loss of productivity, but puts you at risk for making careless errors.

Someone else's emergency

At a local hospital there were 8 patients on the roster and 2 nurses scheduled with no other help. "Looks like it will be a quiet night," commented Teresa, one of the scheduled nurses. Teresa jumped right into her paperwork and assignments. Leslie, the other scheduled nurse, was excited that all of her patients were in stable condition. She chose to delay attending to her paperwork. "After all," she said, "I have all night." Leslie decided to spend her time planning her next vacation. At 4am, Leslie began her patient charting, but within moments, one of her patients took a turn for the worse. She needed to focus on that emergency. At 6am, Leslie's patient was finally stable, but she didn't have enough time to finish her work before the day staff was going to show up. In a panic, she asked Teresa for help. Teresa's reply, "Sorry, but I need to get home on time for my children."

- Don't wait until the last minute to get things done.
- If time permits, then you can consider helping a co-worker.
- If you have a previous commitment, then you can't let your time be taken because of someone else's choices.

We are given the same amount of time each day, and it's important to use our time properly.

Procrastination

Have you ever had something to do that you didn't want to do and just said, "I will do it later." If you do that often enough, the many little things you are putting off suddenly turn into a big mess. My son came home from work and tossed his shirt on the back of the sofa and his bag on the counter. He finished eating supper and left his shoes in the kitchen and his mail on the table. He then proceeded to the computer room to check his emails and left his glass on the desk. I reminded him he needed to take the trash out. He sat on the sofa to rest a minute and realized he was late picking up his girlfriend from work. As he ran out the door, he promised to take care of his mess when he returned home. When morning came, the mess was still there. He had forgotten to take care of it, and to make matters worse, there was no time in the morning because he had overslept and was late for work.

Now, I can just imagine that some of you parents are sighing in shared frustration. Think for a moment about coming home from work so tired that you leave the mail unopened on the counter and the shopping bags on the floor, so that you can quickly get supper ready. After the family eats, your attention is turned to helping your child with their homework. As they are doing their homework, you remember that you need to balance your checkbook, but you are too tired and will do it later. As you are sitting down for a moment, you remember that you forgot to wash laundry. That's ok, you will do it later. As you can see, many of us are guilty of procrastinating too. The sad thing is that each thing only takes a few moments to do, but as each task gets pushed aside, the mess becomes bigger and takes longer to manage when you finally take the time.

My brother is a psychologist, I asked him why people procrastinate. His reply was that some things we just don't consider a priority and other things we just really don't want to do. For tasks that only take a few moments, it is better to put things away or take care of them immediately so that we avoid big mess and save time.

Worksheet

What would you say is the biggest thing that takes your time?

_____

_____

_____

_____

_____

Have you ever experienced a situation where a meeting or gathering took too much of your time?

_____

_____

_____

_____

_____

How have you handled "someone else's emergency" in the past?

_____

_____

_____

_____

_____

What would be the first thing that you would implement to get organized immediately?

_____

_____

_____

_____

_____

What is one thing that you may need time to work through?

_____

_____

_____

_____

_____

Chapter 3
It's Okay to Say NO

Too Many Commitments

Do you feel that you have too many commitments and no time for yourself? Do you often feel guilty and volunteer for everything and then feel frustrated that you didn't say "no"? Are you involved with many activities, but neglecting important responsibilities? Here are some common situations to consider when you may feel the need to take on a new commitment, but need to learn to turn that commitment down.

Volunteering

I love to volunteer. I used to say "yes" to almost every volunteer opportunity, but I began to feel stretched and stressed and was no longer enjoying it. I wanted to help, but realized it had a price tag: my time. I would allow people to make me feel guilty for saying no to "helping them." When my children were in elementary school, I would often help out in the school office or classroom. I had been a stay-at-home mom, so I didn't mind. I was annoyed at the moms who stood in the parking lot and gossiped about problems in the school. I felt that they needed to help instead of complain.

One day I decided to stay home and clean my house instead of helping out at the school. I was spending so much time at the school that my home was being neglected. I received a phone call later that morning from the school, the conversation began like this, "Lisa, what are you doing today?" and my reply was "nothing." I didn't put enough value in cleaning my home. The school principal then proceeded to tell me that one of their teachers was out sick and that I was needed to substitute. I politely declined. He said he couldn't believe that I would leave them in such a bind. I felt guilty. I came to realize that if I didn't say no to them, then I was saying no to myself and my family. I also realized the necessity of rest and a Sabbath time.

If you keep running non-stop, you can burn out and lose your enthusiasm for what you are doing. A pastor's wife told me years ago that I should tell people "I already have plans." It doesn't matter if your plans are sitting on the sofa, fishing, or cleaning house. That's what you want to do. I realized that I was going to have to say no to something, and I didn't want it to be my family or household.

Extra-curricular activities

When my oldest was elementary school age, I had struggled with the thought that all of my son's friends were very athletic. My son had no interest in sports. I enrolled my son in baseball, thinking that my husband would take him to the practices and games. My husband's schedule at work increased and he was unable to take our son to the practices. The responsibility was now mine, despite my already busy schedule.

Every practice, my son would be in outfield chasing bugs rather than participating in the game. Of course, this annoyed the coach. On one specific game, he was wiggly and would not sit down in the dugout. I walked to the dugout and asked him, "Why are you not sitting down?" His reply, "I have a frog in my pocket!" I quickly realized that my husband and I did not have time in our schedule for baseball and our son was not interested in baseball. No one benefitted from the baseball, so there was no reason to keep him in the sport. Don't waste precious time that can be used on something else.

If you have more than one child and they are interested in different activities consider the following suggestion from another mom. Mary asked each of her three children to name one favorite activity. She then announced that in the fall that one child would participate in gymnastics, in the spring another child would participate in baseball and in the summer another would participate in swim. It is important for children to understand at an early age how to compromise with one another. This helped Mary not feel stressed out in going in three different directions. The same guidelines apply to adults. We must also choose what activities we would like to do first, and then as time permits, we can switch to a different activity. Be careful with how many extra-curricular activities you become involved with. Something that can start off as a fun activity can become stressful if we are not taking care of the things that are important such as homework or housework.

Worksheet

Do you have difficulty saying no?

_____

_____

_____

_____

_____

Describe a situation where you should have said no?

_____

_____

_____

_____

How do you relate to this statement, "I came to realize that if I didn't say no to them, then I was saying no to myself or my family"?

_____

_____

_____

_____

_____

Chapter 4
Delegating Household Chores

Too Much To Do

Do you feel like you have too much to do between school and job by day and homework and dishes by night? Do you feel it is difficult to manage working, cooking, washing the dishes, doing the laundry, taking kids to soccer practice, going grocery shopping, and keeping the house clean? What about just wanting to take a nap? Does it sometimes seem that things never get done?

In the business community, we all know what it means to delegate. Whenever possible, it is better to let someone help you. You may find that one of your employees is extremely talented in an area that he or she may not have been hired to do. Instead of struggling to take care of too many things, allow them to work in their strengths.

I was a stay at home mom until my children went to school. I thought that I would simply work while they were at school, but I didn't realize that I would only have the evenings and weekends to fulfill my household obligations. I was exhausted in the evenings, and it took all my energy to cook and help my children with their homework. I needed a plan. One day, I was listening to a family counselor on the radio and liked some of his suggestions on delegating chores to your children. I began to think, "How can I apply this to my household?" I reasoned that anything my children did was better than me doing nothing. After all, the raising of our children is not just about reading, writing, and arithmetic, but is also about manners, life skills, and being self sufficient. Here is what I did.

Tips for delegating household chores to children:

- Each child had one chore in the evening (ex. take out the trash, unload the dishes, or fold laundry).
- Before bed, everyone had to pick up their mess (ex. no shoes or toys in the living room or kitchen).
- Assign weekly chores. One of my children preferred to vacuum and dust while my other child agreed to clean the bathroom sink, tub, and toilet. Now, in the beginning, they didn't do a great job, but it was better than me not being able to do it at all. In time, they became proficient in their chores and I rewarded them with allowance.

I am proud to announce that my sons, ages 19 and 21 as of this writing, are well trained with healthy habits. I haven't cleaned my house alone for over 12 years. If you don't have children in your home and your finances permit it, then consider hiring someone to come in and help. You may also consider trading chores with a friend or spouse. I began to offer to pick up a few things at the grocery for my neighbor and would occasionally bring over supper to my neighbor. After awhile, she began to do the same for me. What a time saver. When my boys were young, I would ask my husband, "Do you want to clean the kitchen or get the boys ready for bed." He always chose getting the boys ready for bed; this was good for me because I enjoyed the quiet time in the kitchen.

Worksheet

How do you feel about letting your children help you with chores?

_____

_____

_____

_____

_____

_____

What chores will you begin implementing?

_____

_____

_____

_____

_____

What would stop you from asking others to "trade chores"?

_____

_____

_____

_____

Chapter 5
All Those Errands

Too many places to go

Are you constantly running around taking care of different errands? Do errands seem endless and time consuming? How do you take care of all the things that you need to do without feeling like you are "running around"?

One day I went to the grocery to pick up stamps and rice; my store has an ATM that dispenses stamps. While there, I decided to buy all my groceries for the week, but I didn't have a list. After getting home, spending over $100, and realizing that I didn't need milk, I noticed that I completely forgot about the stamps. I had to make another trip to get stamps. If I would have had a list, I would have saved time and money by not making repeat purchases and errands.

For many people who operate home-based businesses or who are stay-at-home parents, running errands can provide a welcome opportunity to get out for awhile. One of my friends enjoys running at least one errand a day. She likes to change up her schedule and get away from the "four walls." Another friend prefers to do her shopping online to avoid running errands. I, on the other hand, would prefer to knock them all out in one day and maximize my time in the "four walls." It's up to you as to how you take care of errands, and I will address the daily versus weekly option and help you learn how to maximize your time.

Tips for running errands:

- Have a list of all the places you need to go and things you need to do for the week (ex. going to the post office, grocery, or insurance agent's office).
- Keep a list of all the things you need to purchase for the week
- Be sure to keep your list in a consistent location.
- For daily errands: Look at your calendar and lists to decide when you will run the errand. You may also choose to run an errand before or after work or an appointment.
- For weekly errands: Map out where all the stops will be. You will want to avoid zigzagging; this wastes time. Make your stops along the way in the same part of town or on the same side of the highway and then work your way back.
- Set a date on your calendar for the days and times you plan on taking care of your errands.

I usually go to the grocery store every two weeks except for a weekly trip to get fresh produce and milk. In order to avoid extra trips to the grocery store, you need to have a plan.

Tips for shopping and meal planning

- Create a tentative menu of about 14 different meals. It doesn't matter if you repeat a few meal options. You don't even have to lock down the day that you will fix the meal; you just need to have a list of options.
- Make your grocery list according to the items you will need to prepare each meal. Add quick snacks and other food to the list for additional eating times such as breakfast and lunch. If you like to entertain, have on hand ingredients for a special appetizer.
- Include non-food items such as cleaning products, tissues, and toiletries on your list. If you do not have a running list of these items, you may need to walk around your home and do inventory.
- As you run low on certain grocery items, make a list for your next trip. I use a dry-erase board on the side of my refrigerator. It doesn't matter what means you use to keep your list, just be consistent. If you use a notepad by the phone, then let that always be the place. The next time you need to go the store, you will know what to buy or be able to hand the list to a family member or friend. They will have the ability to get what is needed.

No matter which way you choose to take care of errands, it will be beneficial to be prepared and organized.

Worksheet

What are your preferences on running errands?

_____

_____

_____

_____

_____

Was there a tip presented in this chapter that you hadn't thought of?

_____

_____

_____

_____

_____

_____

Which suggestion do you feel is right for you?

_____

_____

_____

_____

_____

Chapter 6
Making the Most of Time

Give me back Saturday

Do you work all week? Do you dread Saturdays because of all the housework, laundry, and errands you must do? To take back your Saturday, you will need a plan.

When I was a newlywed, many of my friends spent all day Saturday doing laundry, cleaning house, and going to the grocery. This did not seem like a fun way to spend the day, especially since we went to church on Sunday. I heard a family psychologist on the radio suggest to do small chores all throughout the week. His example was while you were brushing your teeth, you could swish that toilet. Whereas toilets and teeth was not a good combination, this was one of those life changing ideas that I ran with. There are many things that we need to do that only take a few moments of our time. I realized that there were other pieces of extra time that I could utilize more efficiently. Extra time away from the home or office is not something that is scheduled on your calendar, but it always manages to find a place in your day.

Example of extra time:

- Riding the bus to work
- Waiting at the doctor's office
- Your child's piano or sports practice
- Time before a meeting or extra time between college classes
- Unexpected meeting cancellations

When I know that I could have these moments of extra time available, I bring things to do with me.

Examples of things to do during extra time:

- A book to read for pleasure or continuing education
- Check book to balance
- Mending or needlework
- Reports to make notes on
- Letters to write or emails to respond to
- Nearby errands to run
- Relax

People used to talk about multi-tasking. I heard on the radio that multi-tasking is not always efficient, but I have found that, at home, there are many opportunities to do two things at once.

Tips for multitasking at home:

- Wash one load of clothes in the morning while the coffee is brewing. Before I leave the house, I put the wet clothes in the dryer.
- Fold the laundry while the children are doing homework.

- Exercise during your favorite show.
- Do one chore each day. Before leaving for work in the morning, swish the toilets, and in the evening, wipe the bathroom counters or sort paperwork. The next day, you could dust the living room or tighten a door hinge. Each chore takes only a few minutes twice a day.

By utilizing just a few of these tips, you can take back your Saturday and have time for the things that matter.

Worksheet

Are your "days off" consumed with things to do?

_____

_____

_____

_____

_____

_____

Are the suggested tips things that you would like to try?

_____

_____

_____

_____

_____

What do you do on your "day off" that could be accomplished a different time?

_____

_____

_____

_____

_____

Chapter 7
Organizing Your Time

Setting up a calendar and lists

Have you ever heard someone say "I don't need a calendar; it's all in my head"? On the other hand, have you ever forgotten an appointment or were late because you thought an appointment was at a different time or day? I jokingly mentioned to a supervisor, "You sure are becoming forgetful!" Her reply was that she wasn't forgetful; she just had too many things to remember. You see, sometimes it is not easy to remember everything—especially with our busy lives. We all have the same amount of time in a day, but it is how we choose to use that time that makes all the difference.

Using a calendar and making check lists can help you eliminate forgotten or late appointments and find the time to do the things you need to do or want to do. When things are written down; you can relax because you don't have to worry about keeping "it all in your head."

You can keep a paper or electronic calendar, but don't use both. When you duplicate your calendar efforts, you risk mistakes. Here is how you can begin setting and using a calendar and lists:

24 Tips for organizing your time:

1. **Record all appointments.** This includes meetings, medical/dental appointments, baseball practices, date reports are due, or special celebrations.
2. **Allow preparation time.** If a meeting or special celebration is coming up, be sure to schedule time to get prepared, shop, or study, if necessary.
3. **Cushion time:** Give yourself extra time for any particularly important meetings or tasks. This allows for interruptions so that your schedule does not back up if an appointment is delayed or you are stuck in line at the store.
4. **Avoid saying "yes."** If you don't have your calendar with you, avoid making commitments; you don't know what you may already have scheduled for that day.
5. **Avoid overbooking.** When you schedule too many activities, meetings, or classes for yourself or your children, you will feel rushed and stressed
6. **Make a list of your daily routines.** Make both a morning and an evening need-to-do list and schedule time for those list into your calendar. Routines such as getting dressed, preparing lunches, packing book bags, and cleaning the kitchen should be included. It may seem funny to write down "get dressed," but it is not something that happens immediately for parents who home school or people who work from home. In the evening, consider adding homework with your children, mealtime, extracurricular activities, setting out clean clothes, checking meeting notes, or filling up the car with gas to your list. When a last-minute appointment or event comes up, you will be ready with a list of what is already taking up your time.
7. **Create a list of must-do projects.** Things on this list should be things that you need to do daily, weekly, and monthly.

8. **Have a list of things you want to do.** This will include updates on your home or office, furthering your education by reading, mending, or catching up on paperwork and emails in addition to fun stuff. When you see the extra time in your schedule, even if it's just a few minutes, you will be able to do one of the items. Some things will take just a short time to accomplish, and others may take longer. It will be such a relief and pleasure to be able to check things off that you wanted to do.

9. **Set aside time for yourself.** We spend most of our time taking care of things we need to do. Put time on your calendar for things you want to do. This may be playing golf, reading a book, or painting a room. Take care of things that are on your list that you want to do. Give those priorities weight as well.

10. **Make a habit of checking your calendar.** Check before you go to bed at night because you may need to wake up earlier or get to sleep in later depending on what your calendar and lists show. In the morning, as you begin the focus of your day, review the priorities of duties that need to be done. As the day progresses, check off what you have completed. This will help you maintain credibility with those who depend on you to accomplish goals for your family or business and give you a great sense of pride and accomplishment.

11. **Pack your bag.** After you check your calendar, pack your bag. Whether it is a briefcase or a diaper bag, packing your bag with necessary items the night before can save time.

12. **Establish planning time.** Set aside a time once a week for planning. This will give your week productivity and purpose. Even if it is just for fun.

13. **Keep a notepad.** Keep a notebook (either paper or electronically) close by to jot down notes you want to

remember throughout the day. This helps to keep you focused on what you are working on and prevents you from staying awake at night thinking about what you need to do.

14. **Maximize your free time.** Keep small tasks with you that you can do when you have unexpected free time (ex. writing notes or balancing the checkbook). This is also a good time to catch up on your reading.

15. **By-pass procrastination.** Instead of procrastinating those dreaded projects, schedule time on your calendar to get them done.

16. **Delegate.** There are many items that you may want to let someone else help you accomplish. This will create more time in your schedule.

17. **Plan your errands.** Avoid wasting time travelling by planning time on your calendar for when you will take care of errands and shopping.

18. **Chores.** Break up weekly chores to one a day, instead of taking your whole day off to do chores.

19. **Take control of your phone.** If you are not waiting for a call, then turn off the ringer. If you are waiting for a call, utilize your caller ID. Text messaging is a very quick effective way to communicate quickly while avoiding the time trap of chatting.

20. **Set computer time.** Computers have a way of taking up a lot of time. Set aside a time twice a day to check your emails. Set a timer for a certain number of minutes and stick to emails or computer related tasks (ex. banking). Avoid the social sites.

21. **Are you a morning person or a night person.** When you know your body's preferences, you can schedule the more tedious tasks for your best time. I work better on

bookkeeping and writing in the morning, but some people are more alert in the evening hours.

22. **Avoid fatigue.** To work more effectively, take short breaks and eat healthy snacks to refresh and refuel.
23. **Avoid bouncing in between projects.** Stay focused on the task at hand. Handle one piece of paper at a time and give it your full attention.
24. **Always make time to rest.** We can't be as productive or peaceful as we'd like if we are tired.

Additional Time Tips

If you find that you are frequently late, then consider a reverse time line. Here is an example of what one would look like for me:

Reverse time line

- **12:30pm** appointment
- **12:05pm** leave for appointment (it takes 15 minutes to drive, and you should allow for last-minute delays)
- **11:25am** get dressed and ready (It takes me about 25 minutes to get dressed, and that allows for last-minute distractions).
- **11:15am** put away paperwork
- **9:30-11:15am** 1 hour and 45 minutes for paperwork (use a timer to not lose track of time).
- **9:00-9:30am** conference call
- **8:35-8:55am** exercise
- **8:00-8:30am** devotional time
- **7:30-8:00am** fix coffee, wash load of laundry, look at calendar
- **7:15am** alarm clock rings

This reverse time line works well for any kind of schedule. The most important thing is to make a plan and write it down of things that need to be accomplished to know how much time you need.

Remember that keeping a calendar and lists will keep you from running in too many directions. Lists will help you maintain your focus so that what you do is productive and relaxing.

Worksheet

Are you the type that likes to use calendars and lists?

_____

_____

_____

_____

_____

_____

_____

_____

_____

Did this chapter give you something to think about?

_____

_____

_____

_____

_____

_____

_____

_____

_____

What did you think of the "reverse time line"?

_____

_____

_____

_____

_____

_____

_____

_____

Considering your schedule, which tips will you use for yourself?

_____

_____

_____

_____

_____

_____

_____

_____

_____

_____

Chapter 8
Organizing Excuses

Why you think you don't have time for this

S ome people defend their clutter. If you are one of those people, then ask yourself these questions: Have I lost time looking for things or paperwork? Have I gone to the store to buy something that I knew I had, but couldn't find? Have I hesitated to invite company over because the house was a mess? Have I missed a birthday party or special event because I didn't remember the invitation was in the bottom of the pile of paper?

But I might need that!

Have you ever purchased and kept "sale" items over the years? Do you have clothes in your closet that you are saving until you lose weight? Have you ever held onto un-used gifts, despite the fact that you can't find a current purpose for them? I'm also sure that when questioned about whether or not you should keep these things, a familiar phrase comes to your mind: "I might need that."

Remember the Y2K scare? Terror struck the hearts of many people around the world as they stocked their garages with can goods in preparation for the end of civilization! There was a man who purchased multiple years worth of canned goods. He even hired someone to build an extra pantry to store all of the food and supplies. It would not have been a bad situation except that the food he stored wasn't necessarily what he ate on a regular basis. He eventually gave much of the food away. It's ok to want to save something that you may need, but you should consider purging some items to make room for the things you love and use.

I can fix that—one day!

Have you ever broke a favorite plate and wanted to fix it? Do you have a broken VCR that you want to repair? I had a client who complained that she couldn't have company over because of all the excess clutter in her home. She never wanted to throw anything away that was broken because she was going to fix it one day. Like many problem messes, this one had started off small with her daughter's broken doll. My client, certain that she would fix it, set it aside in a corner of the living room on a table. Next, a bowl broke, and then a cell phone. The CD player quit working, and a piece of furniture lost a leg. Before she knew it, an entire corner of the living room was piled up with items that "needed fixing." She could no longer entertain company in her once-beautiful living room because of all these would-be projects.

Is it worth fixing? – Questions to ask yourself:

- Do you have the time to fix it?
- Do you have the money to fix it?
- Is the item outdated?
- Does it cost more to repair than it does to replace it?
- Think of the space that you are currently using to store these broken items. Could that space be used more efficiently?

I realize that there are people who feel guilty about throwing things away, but the inconvenience of holding onto those items can, by far, outweigh the guilt. You may consider donating to a place that can repair the item.

It belonged to my mother—and other sentimental excuses

Have you ever kept a vase or an article of clothing that reminded you of a fond time and place? Did you ever receive an ugly shirt from a well-loved aunt? Does keeping certain items make you feel happy? A co-worker of mine told me that her dad had recently passed away (her mom passed away a couple of years ago). She and her brother inherited the whole house of furniture and things. In order to get the house sold, she and her brother emptied the house into their garages. She was completely overwhelmed with the decisions of what to do with everything. There were so many things that she wanted to keep that were reminders of her family and childhood. It was understandable to want to keep those favorite memories, but almost impossible to store it all. Here are some guidelines in helping you to make the decisions on what to keep.

Which memories to keep?

- Decide which items you want to keep and try not to duplicate your existing materials. If you want the dining room table, you may need to sell or give away your current one. If your blender is running fine, but you would like a second one for those "just in case" moments, then you need to decide if you truly have room.
- Decide which items will be given away to other family and friends. Contact them and schedule a time for them to come and pick up the item.
- You may choose to keep a few personal effects such as a favorite suit. Have these properly packed and stored.
- Consider the cost of storing the extra items?
- If an item is sentimental but you do not want to keep it, take photos of it before you get rid of it.
- Do you have room to display or store items such as porcelain collectibles?
- Talk to an attorney and accountant concerning the paperwork that your parent had saved.

Keep in mind that these are only suggestions. There are no rules on the grieving process. I chose to save a few of my mom's things when she passed, but my dad chose not to. Give yourself time. You may just want to keep things in storage for awhile.

I know where everything is!

Have you ever said, "I know it's a mess, but I know where everything is"?

I have seen offices piled with paper and clients who have said to me, "I know where everything is." I had a client once who had asked me to come and help her get organized. She had a home-based business and had papers stored throughout the house, but she did want to get organized. I suggested that we start in the office. The next day, we chose to organize the kitchen, and there, under a large pile, were two checks—one for a few thousand dollars and another for a few hundred dollars, not to mention some cash. She had forgotten all about it. The reality was that she didn't remember where everything was at all.

Many people are apprehensive about getting organized because they don't want to put everything in a file cabinet for fear of losing it. The good news is that there are several ways of filing and organizing.

I just hate to throw things away!

Another common excuse I hear is "I hate to throw stuff away!" Many people have a lot of guilt about getting rid of what they perceive to be useful or about contributing to the landfills. The good news is that unless an item poses a health hazard, you may have other options.

4 things to do with unwanted items:

1. Sell it at a garage sale, an online site or a consignment store.
2. Donate it to your favorite charity
3. Recycle it

4. Give it away to someone who wants it. (Your trash may be someone else's treasure.)

Once you have made peace with discarding unused items, you will be able to enjoy your space, be more productive, locate important items, and free up your time for the things that matter.

Worksheet

Have you ever found yourself using any of the excuses in this chapter?

_____

_____

_____

_____

_____

_____

_____

_____

_____

Which areas may be a problem for you to overcome? Why?

_____

_____

_____

_____

_____

_____

_____

_____

_____

Which questions made sense?

_____

_____

_____

_____

_____

_____

_____

_____

_____

What areas will you begin working on?

_____

_____

_____

_____

_____

_____

_____

_____

_____

Chapter 9
How Much Stuff Do You Have?

Do you have more than one junk drawer? Do you rent a storage unit for all of your extra stuff? Now, I am not against having extra closets and storage, but if you are running out of drawers and closets to use, then maybe it's time to purge. What is in that junk drawer anyway? Can you find the twist ties, batteries, or matches, or are they in the other junk drawer? How about those closets? Seriously, when was the last time you made your way to the back of your closet and wore those red pants? Do your children really play with all their 36 dolls and 72 cars? How long did you dig around among dozens of shirts before you grabbed the same one you always wear? What about the forgotten dress that doesn't fit? Can you find the receipt to return that dress?

19 questions to ask yourself when you have too much stuff:

1. If you can't find it, then how can you use it?
2. Do you need it?
3. When will you ever use it?
4. How long has it been since you used it?
5. If you were moving, would you pay to move it?

6. If you got rid of it, what's the worst that would happen & could you retrieve it again?
7. Is the information obsolete?
8. Are you legally required to keep it?
9. Would you buy it again?
10. How many pieces do you really need to keep?
11. Are you keeping it because someone gave it to you?
12. Will you ever find the time to complete all those craft projects or read those magazines?
13. Is it broken and will the cost of repairing justify the cost of keeping it?
14. How long will it be before you bring those clothes and dishes to your aunt, who lives in another state?
15. Do those jeans still fit?
16. Do you remember which magazine has your favorite article in it?
17. Do you have room in your home or office, or do you need to buy more space?
18. If you choose to store it, then how much is it costing to keep and will you ever really make the time to get back to it?
19. Are you ever going to enjoy it again and will you be able to find it?

You must be willing and ready to release the things that could be unnecessary. Once you have made that decision, you may feel like asking yourself this question: "How do I get started?

Worksheet

Did you relate to this chapter?

_____

_____

_____

_____

_____

_____

Which of the 19 questions will you use as a guide to getting organized?

_____

_____

_____

_____

_____

_____

Are you ready to give up some stuff?

_____

_____

_____

Chapter 10
Organizing Your Paper

Can you Go Green?

Are you overwhelmed by your mail and other paperwork? Have you ever wondered how, with all the talk about "going green" and "saving the planet," you still deal with so much paperwork? It is amazing that even with today's technology, paperwork is still a big part of our lives. Everything that is junk mail needs to be tossed or recycled. Unless you have some kind of strategy for paperwork, it will take on a life of its own. It will grow, follow you, and eventually engulf your entire home or office.

My favorite tip for dealing with paperwork comes from my friend Tiffany. The first time I went to her home, I noticed that it was spotless—no paper or mail to be seen. Tiffany said the secret to her neat home was that she takes care of mail right away. This strategy keeps paperwork from getting out of control.

Now, I consider myself organized, but I used to have mail and paperwork on my table. My priority was not the mail; I like to do the dishes right away. Some women need to do their laundry right away and others like to make their beds. I don't like to make my bed. I just close the door to the room.

However, I've realized that you will eventually do the laundry and the dishes, but your mail, it keeps growing if you ignore it. The longer you ignore it, the more anxiety you feel and the longer it will take for you to deal with it.

Many of my clients just avoid the mail and the incoming paperwork. The problem is that once they start sorting and organizing their paperwork, they find expired checks, late bills, or invitations to past events.

Quick tips for organizing incoming paperwork and mail

1. **Sort:** Avoid the temptation to stop and read everything. It seems simple, but once you get in the habit of sorting everything into piles for the trash and that need attention, your mail and incoming paperwork will never get out of control again.
2. **Purge:** Toss, shred, or recycle the obvious trash and relocate non-paper items. For paperwork that you are not sure if you should keep or discard consider the following questions: If you got rid of it, what's the worst that would happen? Could you retrieve it again? Is the information obsolete? Are you legally required to keep it? If you are unsure of the answers to any of these questions, contact your accountant or attorney for guidelines.
3. **Group** like item that make it past the initial trash sort.

    a. **To do:** invitations, bills to pay, calls to the insurance company. For items that need action, such as paying a bill or making a phone call, make a list of things to do and schedule time on your calendar to follow through on those items. Do not just place the paper in a pile to get lost or forgotten.

b. **To Read/Coupons:** These are items that do not need your attention now, but when you have the time to read or use.

c. **Follow-up:** Receipts for reservation for a week at the beach, prescription to call and see if it was ready to pick up. This group is for items that you have already taken action on and that may need a follow-up call or email. Make a list of things you need to do and schedule time on your calendar to follow through on them. Do not just place the paper in a pile to get lost or forgotten.

d. **To be Filed:** Future reference items like bank statements and utility bills. Since many items may be found online, this category can be used for items such as receipts or for items that will be used for tax purposes.

4. **Assign** a home to paper items by putting papers in their proper file. I do not recommend leaving the paperwork in piles, but choose your favorite type of storage containers. Some of my clients prefer vertical filing while others prefer horizontal filing containers.

5. **Maintain** in order to prevent paperwork from becoming a problem again. It is important to have a maintenance plan. Just as our cars need regular maintenance, your organizational system needs occasional maintenance too. I recommend you sort all incoming mail daily, and then once a year (I like tax time), you conduct a purge of your file drawers or archive locations.

Favorite tips for organizing paper

1. **For storing warranties and manuals:** Warranties and manuals are usually thick and take up a lot of space; to store them, use a plastic container you can keep in the closet.

2. **For storing your child's school work and artwork:** Someone gave me a valuable tip when my children were young. At the end of the week, look at all of your children's art work and school work and only save one piece of paper. At the end of the school quarter, save the best three pieces of paper. This way, at the end of the school year, you will only have twelve pieces of paper to store for keepsake. Discard in a black trash bag when your children aren't looking. Some children may feel upset at seeing their artwork discarded or recycled. This may seem harsh, but if you try to save everything, you may never get around to looking at it again. Another suggestion is to scan the artwork.

3. **For storing legal documents:** For legal documents such as birth certificates, passports, credit card/ banking account numbers or insurance policies, consider storing them in a fire-proof box for safety. This is also useful in the event that you need to take all important documents with you in case of an emergency evacuation such as a hurricane or fire.

4. **Electronic information:** With so much information that is available online and the option of scanning, there is becoming less of a need to store paperwork. In some cases, it will be a personal preference as to what papers to save or not. Consult your accountant if you need guidelines on what to save for tax or legal purposes.

5. **Magazine articles:** After I look at a magazine, I take favorite articles, recipes, or ideas and tear them out and

place them into sheet protectors in a binder or scan them and label the category. This saves space and time when I want to locate and refer to that article later. If I don't have time to look at a magazine, I circle the article of interest on the cover to read later. This helps me to remember why I may have saved the magazine. After I am finished with the magazine, I either donate it to the school or a neighbor or recycle it.

6. **Receipts:** Have you ever bought a pair of pants and realized a week later that they didn't fit. Could you remember where you left the receipt? Did your dishwasher malfunction and you needed your receipt for proof of warranty. For large purchases, it is best to attach the receipt to the manual. For smaller purchases, you could store receipts in a file folder that you should periodically weed. You may want to keep the receipt for clothes for a shorter amount of time than you'd keep the receipt for an appliance. I keep mine in an envelope in my desk drawer.

7. **Bills to be paid:** It is easier to pay bills on pay day when you have all your information in one area. I keep my bills in a desk drawer. That drawer contains all the things that need to be paid and the accounts that will be used to make the payments. This is also a good time to balance your checkbook, whether electronically or paper. Many times automatic deposits and payments and the use of debit cards make it harder to keep your finances organized. Read your statements and make sure all transactions are accurate and yours.

8. **Setting up your filing system:** I purchased a couple of filing systems at a local store that I was going to use for clients. When I brought them home, I noticed that there were important categories missing from the packages. The packages also included what I considered to be irrelevant

categories. Everyone thinks differently when they file paperwork. When you are preparing to file something, ask yourself, "What category will I think of first when I need to retrieve this piece of paper again?" Set up simple categories using one or two relevant words. It must be easy for you to remember so that you can find the document later. An example would be that instead of one folder for vision, a second for dental, and a third one for prescriptions, create one folding using the word medical. Another example would be instead of having a folder for the electric bill and another folder for the water bill and a separate one for the phone bill, you could create one folder for utility bills. Also, don't create words that may make it too difficult for someone else to locate at a later date.

9. **Memories:** Since I am an organizer, I try not to save too many cards, letters, and personal paperwork. For special occasion cards that have been given to me, it either has to make me laugh out loud, cry, or have a handwritten note enclosed for me to consider keeping it. I keep a pretty box in the top of my closet to store these special memories. Remember, if you save too many, then you won't be able to find them or have time to enjoy them.

10. **Cookbooks and recipes:** I love cookbooks, but I realized that if I had too many, then it was harder to store them. Chances are that you have a few favorite cookbooks and a few you hardly ever use. Keep only your favorite cookbooks and donate the rest. Even more of a challenge was storing all those recipes scribbled on pieces of papers of all different sizes. Now I keep all of my loose recipes in a folder next to my cookbooks, since it keeps things neat and tidy. The best place to keep cookbooks and recipes is where you will use them—in the kitchen. For those of you who prefer to be paperless, another great option is to

scan all your favorite recipes and organize them in a folder in your computer according to categories, such as soups, entrees, or desserts.

11. **Unopened mail:** It is best to take care of mail right away, but if you are unable to, then choose a consistent spot to place all incoming mail and paperwork. Some people enjoy having a container for mail by the front door, others prefer a spot on the counter, and still others bring it into the home office. You should try to avoid placing mail in a purse or bag. You may forget that you left it there. The goal is to keep your home neat and remember where you placed the paperwork.

12. **Notepads and check lists:** It is tempting to grab a piece of paper to write notes, but after a while those types of notes just increase your piles of paper. Consider using one place where you can write all notes. If you find yourself away from home or the office, use a pocket notebook or send yourself a quick email through your phone. Also, look online for many more options to make note taking easier. This will help avoid all those scraps of paper.

13. **Medical paperwork:** Store all medical paperwork in a file and store with the explanation of benefit from your insurance company. It is important to know what your insurance paid so as to know what you may still owe.

14. **Utility bills and bank statements:** With so much being online these days, there are many people who opt out of the printed form. Either way, be sure to look at your statements on a regular basis to make sure that all charges and credits are correct.

15. **Do you need to keep it?** Before you decide to toss paperwork, check with your accountant.

I had a friend who owned her own business. She had an office at home for personal use and a separate location for her business. One day she complained that she was just going to take everything in her home office and toss it. She thought if she hadn't touched it, then there was no point in saving it. She gave a second consideration and decided to go through each pile. In an old shoe box, she found a treasury note that was worth thousands of dollars. She was very thankful that she sorted first and did not just dispose of everything. Now, while you may not find money, there may be paperwork of value in your messy piles that you need to save—and plenty of things to toss.

Worksheet

Did this chapter motivate you to want to get organized and if so, how?

_____

_____

_____

_____

_____

What could stop you?

_____

_____

_____

_____

Do you need help in getting started? If so contact us and we would be glad to get you on the right track.

_____

_____

_____

_____

_____

Chapter 11
Favorite Tips to Organize Your Home

Do you ever lose or misplace things in large piles of miscellaneous stuff? Have you ever missed an important event because you could not find the invitation? Do you waste time and money buying items that you know you already own, but have misplaced? Do you feel that you need more hours in a day? Are you embarrassed to have company over because your house is a mess?

I've created a quick list of some of my most effective organizing tips to help you save time and money. Many of my clients are pleased with my tips and I often receive comments such as "Wow, that makes sense!" and "I didn't think about that."

25 Favorite organizing tips:

1. **Put things away.** When you come home, don't leave your shoes in the hallway. When you finish reading a magazine, don't leave it out. When you finish eating a snack, don't leave the wrapper in the living room.
2. **Group like items with like items.** For example, cleaning supplies and office supplies should go in specific locations so that you know where to find them. For example, you could keep your coffee supplies in a cabinet by the coffee

pot. Think of it as a store: you will find that pens are on one aisle, while paper may be on another aisle. Use this same type of system for your home or office.

3. **Assign a home.** Every item should have a home. If an item has its own place and you put things away, you will always know where to find it.

4. **Delegate.** If you don't have time to do everything on your own, then delegate tasks that others are capable of doing. Also, consider sharing tasks with family members or your neighbor.

5. **One a day.** Complete one chore or wash one load of laundry a day. This will prevent the housework from piling up into one big chore day.

6. **Maintenance.** Set aside time once or twice a year to clear out a closet or file cabinet. Take the time to empty it of all the items that are no longer used or needed.

7. **Multitask.** You can exercise or fold a load of laundry while watching TV or helping your children with their homework.

8. **Things to go.** Have a container at the door for items to be returned, given as a gift, or needed for the next trip or errand.

9. **Donations.** Have a box in your closet for items to be donated. When the box is full, make one trip to the donation center.

10. **Take something with you.** When you exit your car or leave a room, take something with you. For example, it is easier to take the trash out of the car as you are exiting than it is to go back later to empty the trash. It takes less time to bring laundry into your bedroom when you are going there to read a book than it does to go back later.

11. **Is it broken?** If an item is broken and you are saving it because you know you will fix it one day, ask yourself this

question, "Is it really worth the time and cost that it would take to fix it?"

12. **Purge.** When you acquire something new, consider getting rid of something older to avoid excess clutter. How many calculators do you need? Do you have room to store it all? Do you remember where the other calculator is? How many pairs of black shoes do you need?

13. **Observe clutter.** When you notice that there is no more room in your refrigerator or file cabinet, take a moment to observe clutter and toss unwanted items. It only takes a few moments and will give you more space and save time later.

14. **Pack your bag.** Whether it is a briefcase or a diaper bag, keeping your bag packed with the necessary items can save you time.

15. **Use a timer.** Timers can help keep you on task and not lose track of time. Set your timer for a certain number of minutes, and when the timer goes off, you are done. This is especially useful when you are checking your emails.

16. **Use lists and calendars.** They will always help to remind you of things you need to do. If you need to call someone, attend a meeting next week, or you are out of milk, then write it down.

17. **Mail.** Go through mail as soon as it comes in and toss the trash. Sort the rest into three possible categories: To be filed (ex. receipts). To do (ex. pay a bill). To Read and Coupons (ex. things that do not require our immediate attention). Whatever mail lands in the "to do" category, make sure you record the day that action needs to be taken in your calendar. I do not recommend leaving the paperwork in piles but choose your favorite type of storage container. Some clients prefer vertical filing while others prefer horizontal filing containers.

18. **Magazines.** Instead of saving a whole magazine for one article, recipe, or picture, cut out the page that you want and place it in a sheet protector in a binder or scan them. The next time you want to look at that article, you will know where to find it.

19. **Photos.** Sort and label photos according to event, family, friends, or by year in a protected box or by scanning to keep history accurate. This way it is easier to reminisce. You may also want to keep the more precious photos. How many photos of the party do you need and do you remember who those people are in the photo?

20. **Children's school work and artwork.** Each week, save your favorite piece of school work or artwork. At the end of each quarter keep your favorite 3 pieces. This way, by the end of the school year, you will only have 12 pieces of paper to store for keepsakes. Discard the rest in a black trash bag when your children are not present. Some children may feel upset at seeing their artwork discarded and recycled. This may seem harsh, but if you try to save everything, you may not know where the paper is or have the time to look for it. Another suggestion is to scan those projects and keepsakes first; that way you can save more of their work.

21. **Monitor computer use.** Computers have a way of taking up a whole lot of time. Set aside time twice a day to check emails. Review the subject line. If time is limited, resist the urge to open non-important emails or visit social networking sites.

22. **Infrequently used items.** Use under-bed containers for storing gift-wrapping or craft supplies. Store seasonal items, long-term paperwork (such as tax returns and home title papers), or hand-me-down clothes in large containers. Make sure that they are clearly labeled; you don't want to

forget what's in there. Store the containers in the closet, under the bed, or in the attic

23. **Use open shelving for children.** Place toys and items they need in clear containers with no lids, so that they can see what they have and put things away with ease.

24. **Buy dual-purpose furniture.** If space is limited in your home or office, take a moment to consider the efficiency of that night stand or writing table that you are about to purchase or may have already have. I use part of my buffet server to store office supplies and reference work.

25. **Can you afford that?** Do you have a time and place for everything? Before you buy something new, consider the cost. Do you have time to maintain it and do you have a place for it?

More favorite tips

- **Bulk storage:** assign a certain closet area to store bulk supplies: dry or canned goods, office or school supplies, and seasonal items. Keep in mind that the best time to stock up is when it is cost effective and when you can forecast a need for those items. If you buy just to buy, then it could turn into clutter.

- **Suitcases and such.** Store your smaller suitcases and traveling accessories inside of your larger suitcases. This will take up less storage space and when it is time for a trip you will be able to locate everything that you need for travelling.

- **Avoid stacking too many containers in a closet.** Consider adding shelves to avoid the mess that comes from needing the container on the bottom of a stack. Label the containers for easy retrieval.

- **Trash.** Keep a small trash can in each room to keep things tidy.

My goal for organizing is to keep things simple. If you take care of things right away, then you will avoid big messes.

Worksheet

What were your favorite tips?

_____

_____

_____

_____

_____

Which ones will you begin using?

_____

_____

_____

_____

_____

What are your thoughts after reading the list?

_____

_____

_____

_____

_____

Chapter 12
Let's Organize

But I have a life or I am not that Type*!*

I was completely overwhelmed at the first organizing workshop that I attended. The details that this woman went into were amazing. I always felt that I was organized, but I was nothing compared to this woman. I like to label containers, but really, who labels everything in the refrigerator? Upon leaving her workshop, I thought, "I have a life."

There are ways to be organized without being a perfectionist—and while still having a life. It depends on your priorities and the time you want to invest in organizing. Another area to consider is your personality type. You may be a left-brained person and love things to be organized and logical, or you may be right brained and very artistic. I was the sister who enjoyed neatness and order. My sister, on the other hand, preferred to do crafts than to spend her time organizing. One day I found myself wishing that I were more creative and my sister wanted to be more organized. We all sometimes wish we were a little like others, but I tell my clients that it is okay that we all have different personalities; that is the reason it is important to help each other. Organizing may be as simple as placing photos in a box according to year or scrapbooking according to each event. The important part of being organized is having a system that allows you to locate what you need, when you need it, and have time for the things that matter.

I had a friend who was never able to sit on her sofa because it was always filled with clean laundry. The coffee table always had old newspapers, and scattered across the floors were multiple pairs of tennis shoes. She called for help one day because she was ready to host a ladies Bible study in her home, but her home was a mess. I decided to go over to her house and assist her in getting organized. First, we put the shoes away in the bedrooms. It didn't matter that the bedrooms were a mess and there was no place set aside in the bedroom for shoes; the point was to get the shoes out of the living room. The second step was to toss trash and place the old newspapers into the recycling bin. Finally, we folded and put away the laundry. The greatest obstacle was not the amount of clutter, but that she was overwhelmed as to where and how to begin organizing. What an "aah" moment for this person! It felt good for her to be able to sit on the sofa and enjoy her living room with a cup of coffee and a friend. Once the living room was cleared, my friend gained the confidence she needed to tackle one closet at a time. We started with the craft closet, then the linen closet, and finally her bedroom closet. While cleaning the closets, we were able to toss, giveaway, and restack her items properly. After the closets were cleared and organized, she then had room to put things away (including the tennis shoes). This was also the beginning of organizing the bedrooms.

When preparing to organize, it is important to set aside an allotment of time. It is amazing what you can accomplish in a half day or even just a half hour. Once you see the results of one small area, then you have the motivation to do more. Don't look at the whole mess. I used to tell my boys to view a room as a clock and find your 12:00 position. Start cleaning at the 12:00 and then move to the 1:00 position until you work your way around the room. To avoid being distracted, don't look at the other areas. When organizing is divided into smaller pieces, it is easier to accomplish.

5 Quick steps to getting organized:

1. Sort: Begin by sorting the items in your room.
2. Purge: Toss the trash or recycle unwanted items and relocate items to their proper rooms and spaces, such as dishes in the kitchen and shoes in the closet.
3. Group: Put like items together, such as office supplies or cleaning products.
4. Assign a home: Put items in a container and then place them in their new location.
5. Maintain: Periodically go through rooms and closets to put things away and toss no longer useful items.

It's amazing how organized your area will seem when items that don't belong are now put in their proper place.

Chapter 13
It's Not Me; It's Them

Words of caution

Is your spouse, roommate, or co-worker a pack rat? Do you feel that if only their mess was picked up, then the house or office would look better? I strongly caution you: Do not touch their stuff.

I decided one day that my husband's desk and dresser were out of control. I was unable to put away his socks due to all his stuff. I began to sort and toss. Anyway he noticed in the trash that I had thrown away a broken piece of plastic. He told me that it was something he had received as a child. I'd also tossed the duplicate copy of our house plans. He was not pleased. We had to come up with compromises. Here is a suggestion as to how you can handle your situation:

- Decide what areas of the house are important to you to remain neat. (For example: kitchen & living room)
- Decide what areas you can give into a little of their clutter. (For example: bedroom & garage)

This may be an oversimplified answer, but it is very important to respect each other's differences in life and to make compromises, while avoiding criticism of the other person.

Worksheet

Did you relate to the example in this chapter?

_____

_____

_____

_____

_____

_____

How do you feel about learning to compromise?

_____

_____

_____

_____

_____

Is this something you may want to work on?

_____

_____

_____

_____

_____

Chapter 14

In and Out of Boxes

Does the thought of moving bring hope for a new beginning or does it bring fear of the overwhelming task of moving all your stuff? The last thing that you want to do is to bring your junk and clutter to your new place or home. And if you are trying to sell your home, then getting rid of the clutter in your home is even more important. It will help you get the best price for your home and sell it the quickest.

I had a client who called an agent to list her home for sale. When the agent came to see her home, he was abrupt and told her that if she cleaned the place up, she might get $127,000. Even though the agent was not as pleasant as my client would have preferred, it motivated my client to get rid of the clutter. Once their home was neat and organized, the house sold for $154,000. What a difference! With a little extra time and money, the profits were big.

Tips for getting your home ready for a move:

- Toss the trash
- Donate or sell items that you no longer need or love
- Put into portable storage all unnecessary items that you want to keep

- Consider having your home staged; certain rooms may need to be repainted; furniture can be rearranged and decorated using your own existing items

Before you plan your move, you should begin the process of de-cluttering and organizing. This will give you fewer things to pack and unpack.

Still in boxes

Let's say that you were not able to de-clutter before you moved. You may not have had the time or you were not sure how much space your next place would have. Well, you moved in six months ago. The move went well and you unpacked almost all the boxes. You and your spouse are both working full time though, and you haven't found the time to finish unpacking everything. Come to think of it, you haven't found the tax folder either. How do you find the time or space to unpack the rest of your things? This is a common dilemma for many families.

5 Tips to help you get out of boxes

- Set aside time one day a week to unpack boxes.
- As you open each box, decide which items are trash. It is amazing what gets thrown into boxes when the movers are packing up your home.
- As you are going through items, decide whether or not you should keep them. If you do not need the item(s),

and there is no place to store them, you should consider donating or selling them.
- When you find items that you treasure or need, take the time to place them in a designated room.
- Once each item is in its designated room, you may want to take another day to put things away properly.

Be sure to look through the boxes one by one, and if you have time, unpack another box. By doing so, you can overcome the feelings of being overwhelmed and see that unpacking can be manageable. Imagine the feeling of progress, knowing that you are completing your move one box at a time.

Worksheet

Was your last move a pleasant experience?

_____

_____

_____

_____

_____

_____

Do you still have unpacked boxes?

_____

_____

_____

_____

_____

_____

Which tips will you use now or for the future?

_____

_____

_____

_____

_____

Chapter 15

Can You Afford That?

I heard a minister say one time, "Can you afford that"? Now a lot of people may think that this comment refers to money, but it's a question that asks much more than that. Can you afford to maintain it?

I have viewed many scenarios of how people justify all their extra belongings. They have many items that they hope to use one day, but they have no room in their home. Some people spend money to buy a bigger house or rent a storage unit to hold all their things. I have many friends who love to hunt, fish, and scrapbook. I know that there is the cost of purchasing their supplies, storing their supplies, time to enjoy their hobby, and then cleaning their supplies before storing it again.

My husband and I purchased a house with a pool. We were so excited to have a home with a pool. What we quickly realized was that you need to clean the pool daily, whether you feel like it or not. A pool can become green very quickly. We were quite surprised by the cost of the chemicals, and it seemed like every summer there was an additional cost of something related to the pool that needed repairing. We had to make room in our shed to store all the extra supplies and chemicals.

As time passed and our schedules changed, the time we spent swimming in the pool lessened, but the time it took us to clean and maintain the pool remained the same. When we bought our next home we decided to not have a pool, but to join a club that featured a pool. Let someone else clean the pool.

5 Questions to ask before making that purchase:

- Do I really need that?
- Do I really want it?
- Where will I place it or store it?
- Can I get rid of something else to make a place for it?
- Do I have time to maintain and enjoy my new purchase?

Once your home or office is organized, then remember that for every new item that you purchase, you will need to find a time and place for it.

Worksheet

How did you feel about the question, "Can you afford that"?

_____

_____

_____

_____

_____

_____

_____

Do you think that this lesson may affect how you acquire new items and what you may do with existing things?

_____

_____

_____

_____

_____

_____

_____

_____

_____

Time and Place for Everything

When people feel time is short, they will leave things where they left them for convenience sake, but that bad habit actually ends up wasting more of your time. I remember a time in my life when my mother was ill and my children were toddlers, and I did not like opening mail. I felt that if I were to open it, then I would have to deal with it and then file it. Days turned into weeks and weeks turned into months and before I knew it, five months of mail had accumulated. Funny thing was that even though I was ignoring it, it was not going away. I called a friend and asked her to babysit my sons so that I could take care of the paperwork. What should have taken only a few minutes each day now took an entire afternoon to organize. On top of the time it took for me to get organized were the fees that I had incurred from late bills. Imagine the embarrassment of almost having your water turned off because you forgot to pay the $28 bill. We waste time by looking for things that were not put away or taken care of right away.

Part of the quest to get organized is the challenge of finding the time to get organized. Since a young girl, I have understood the importance of writing things down, of keeping a calendar and list. Writing down what needs to be done has helped me to focus on the moment instead of what I need to do later.

The stories and examples that I have provided are intended to help you see the importance of having a plan to achieve your goals.

I challenge you to develop new habits of getting organized so that you can have *A Time and Place for Everything.*

About the Author

Lisa Giesler is the energized and self-motivated owner of A Time and Place for Everything, LLC. She enjoys helping people organize their homes, offices and lives in a fun and simple manner as well as helping people unpack and organize their new homes. In today's society, many have recognized the benefits of managing their time and space. A properly organized life increases productivity at work and home, reduces stress, and results in more time to enjoy family and hobbies. There is no job too small or too big for *A Time and Place.*

Her humorous and informative speaking style entertains and encourages while educating those who seek organizational and time management skills. Lisa has enjoyed writing organizing advice for different publications including the *Fort Bend Independent Newspaper.*

Lisa has been involved with the fall festivals for Believer's Life Family Church in New Orleans, Katrina relief with Convoy of Hope, is a board member for SCCHE and a local ABWA, member of NAPO, Faithful Organizers' Speaker Directory, and her local Chamber of Commerce. Lisa has worked on fundraisers for Fort Bend Lawyer's Care and Casa de Esperanza, participated in YMCA Healthy Kids Day, and worked as a mentor for Houston ISD. She is also a volunteer staff member for Faith and Action, located in Washington, D.C.

Her continuing education includes diplomas from the Emerging Leaders Institute, Berean School of the Bible, and various courses in the organizing field. These give Lisa the ability to encourage and lead others to achieve their goals. Lisa holds credentials through the Evangelical Church Alliance.

www.atimeandplace4.com

CPSIA information can be obtained at www.ICGtesting.com
Printed in the USA
LVOW100745230113

316874LV00003B/136/P